My First Book of
PUZZLE FUN

Fran Newman-D'Amico

Dover Publications, Inc.
Garden City, New York

Bibliographical Note

My First Book of Puzzle Fun, first published by Dover Publications, Inc., in 2014,
is a republication of the work originally published by Dover in 2005.

International Standard Book Number

ISBN-13: 978-0-486-77961-4
ISBN-10: 0-486-77961-0

Manufactured in the United States by LSC Communications
77961003   2020
www.doverpublications.com

Note

Welcome to the world of puzzles! There's lots of fun ahead, as you fill in crosswords, search for words, complete mazes, follow the dots, and look for what's the same and what's different. You'll also color by number, find pictures that are exactly alike, use a shape code, and follow the directions for many other puzzle pages. As you make your way through the book, you'll be amused by dancing hippos, skating penguins, a hungry mouse, and many other charming creatures.

If you need help with a puzzle, or if you want to check your answers, look at the Solutions section, which begins on page 53. Don't peek until you've tried your best! When you have finished the puzzles, you can have even more fun by coloring in the pictures with colored pencils, crayons, or markers. Enjoy!

Look carefully at these four cute bears. Find and circle Birthday Bear. He is wearing a striped party hat, sneakers, and a bow.

4

What kind of fish do dogs chase?

◇ = a   ■ = h   ● = f   ⚡ = t

▲ = c   ☆ = i   ♥ = s

___ ___ ___ ___ ___ ___ ___
▲   ◇   ⚡   ●   ☆   ♥   ■

What runs, but never gets out of breath?

◇ = a   ⚡ = t   🌀 = e   ▮ = w   🌙 = r

___ ___ ___ ___ ___
▮   ◇   ⚡   🌀   🌙

Use the shape code to answer each riddle. Write the letters in the blanks to spell out the answers.

All of the hats in this picture ended up on the wrong person! Draw a line from the hat to the person it belongs to.

Each row of pictures tells a little story.
What happened first [1], next [2], and last [3]?
Number the boxes.

These dancing hippos all look pretty much
the same, but only two are exactly the same.
Find and circle these two hippos.

I am the tiniest of birds. It sounds as if
I am humming when I flutter my wings.
Connect the dots to see my picture.

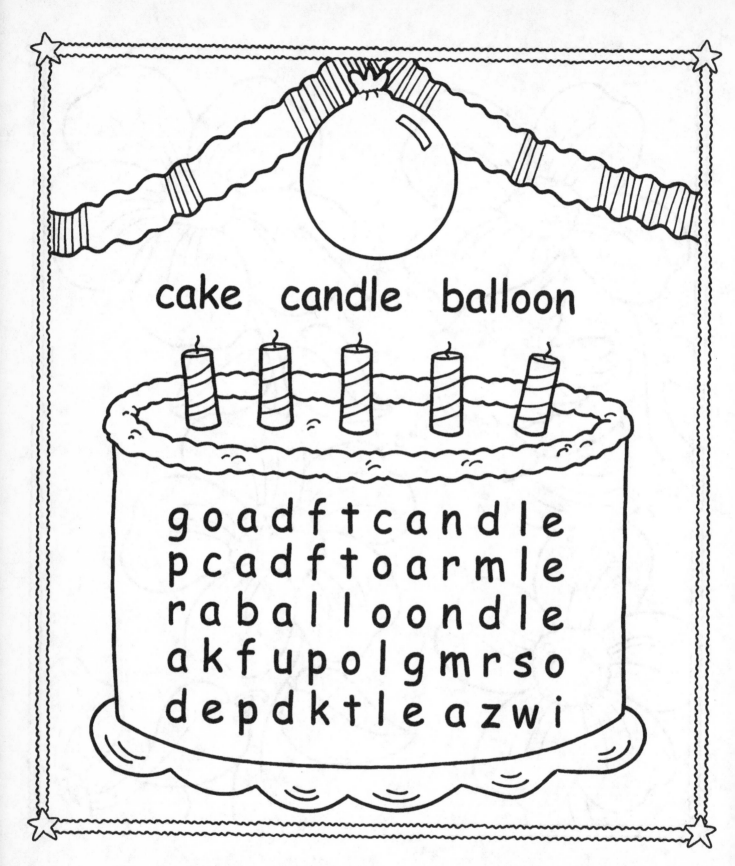

cake   candle   balloon

```
g o a d f t c a n d l e
p c a d f t o a r m l e
r a b a l l o o n d l e
a k f u p o l g m r s o
d e p d k t l e a z w i
```

It's time for a party! Find the three words
above the cake in the puzzle below them.
Circle the words, which go across or down.

Each animal on the left belongs in one of the pictures on the right. Draw a line to match each animal with a picture.

This astronaut is ready to go back to the spaceship. You can help by showing her the path to get there.

12

What is a large group of fish called?

un

du ☐ k

☐ eart

b ☐ ne

d ☐ ll

pai ☐

To answer the question, fill in a letter to spell the name of each picture. Then read the word you have made from top to bottom.

			1 down
2 across		3 down	
		r	
		o	
4 across		o	
		s	
5 across		t	
		e	
		r	

Complete the puzzle by using the picture clues. Write each word where it belongs in the puzzle. One word has been done for you.

2 across

1 down

3 down

5 across

4 across

The number tells you where the word belongs in the puzzle.

START

END

Peggy sees some coins! Help her find the path to the piggy bank. Then, in the blank space in the bank, write how much money she found.

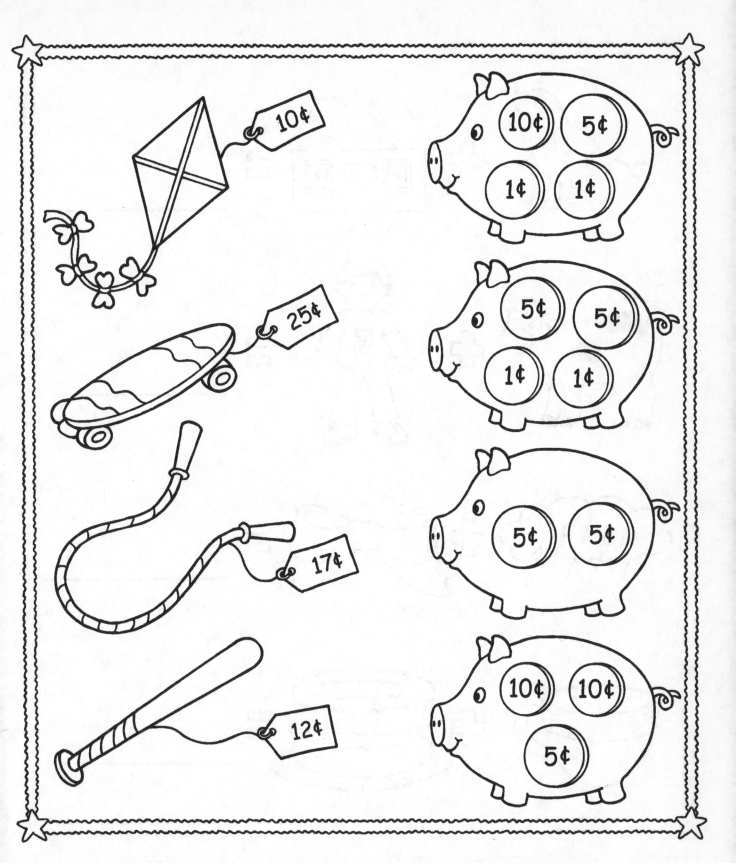

Count the money in each piggy bank.
Then draw a line from each toy to the bank
that has the amount that the toy costs.

The pictures in each pair, added together, make a new word. Figure out the words for each pair and write the new word in the blank.

Have some circus fun! Color the 7 circles red. Color the 7 squares yellow. Color the 7 triangles green. Then color the rest of the picture.

19

Connect the dots from 1 to 21 and you will see
an animal that lives in a land of snow and ice.

These animals in a row look alike, but they're not! Put an X on the cow, the pig, and the rooster that is not the same as the others.

These funny clowns are missing something—
their noses and hats! You can help by
drawing a hat and a nose on each clown.

tent

pqabwtentclo
guadsbaarlci
fabaedognoln
acfwaolgmwok
rkpelephanti

elephant

clown

seal

dog

Here are five things seen at a circus. Circle the names of these things in the puzzle. The words go across and down. Good luck!

Poor bear—half of him is missing! You can help him by drawing in his other half.

Use the picture clues to find and
circle 7 things hidden on this page.

These animals would love to find their tails!
Draw a line from each animal to its tail
and you will make them very happy!

Everyone's having fun at Megan's party! Color the picture: 1=red, 2=yellow, 3=blue, 4=orange, 5=green, 6=brown, 7=pink, and 8=purple.

What goes up when the rain comes down?

= m = r = b = a

= u = l = e

___ ___ ___ ___ ___ ___ ___ ___ ___

What band never makes music?

= b = u = e = r

___ ___ ___ ___ ___ ___

Use the picture code to write the letters in the blanks and solve the riddles.

28

These penguins are enjoying skating on the frozen pond. Two of the penguins are exactly alike. Find them and circle them.

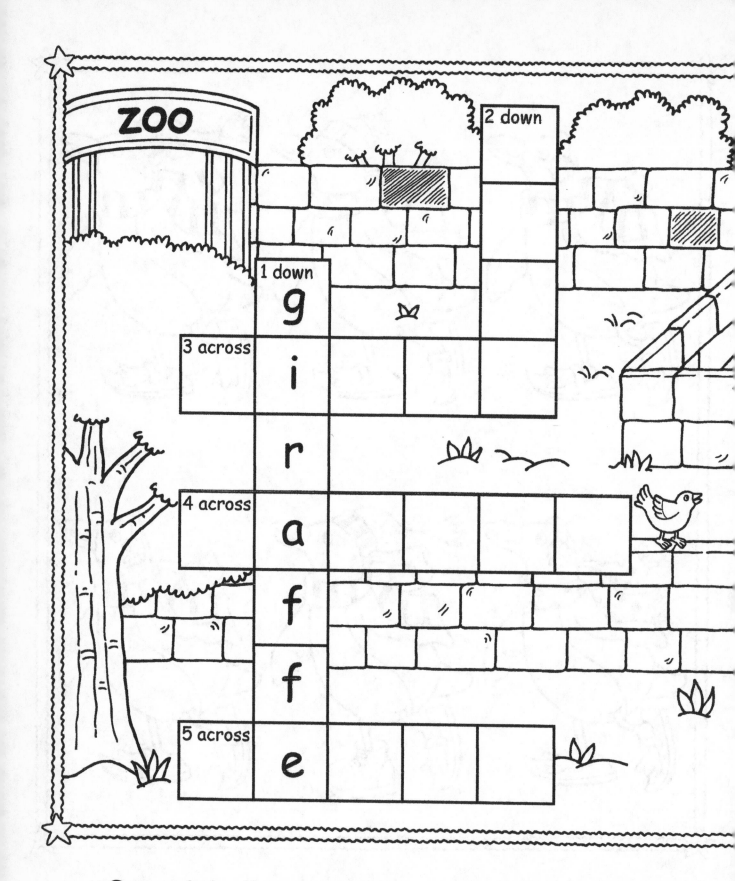

ZOO

2 down

1 down
g
i
r
a
f
f
e

3 across

4 across

5 across

Complete the puzzle by using the picture clues. Write each word where it belongs in the puzzle. One word has been done for you.

The numbers tell you where
the words go in the puzzle.

These underwater friends have found
something at the bottom of the sea.
Connect the dots to see what it is.

Here's a silly picture of a fish
that is fishing! Put an **F** on all of the
things that begin with the letter "F."

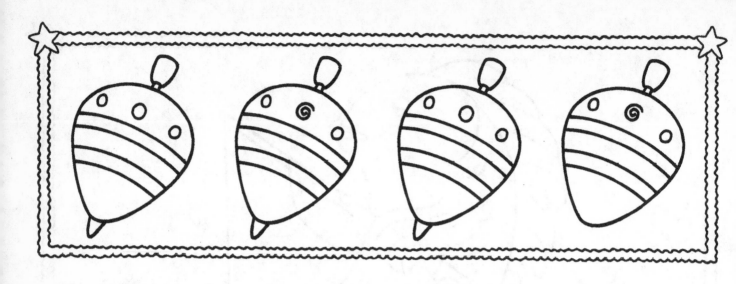

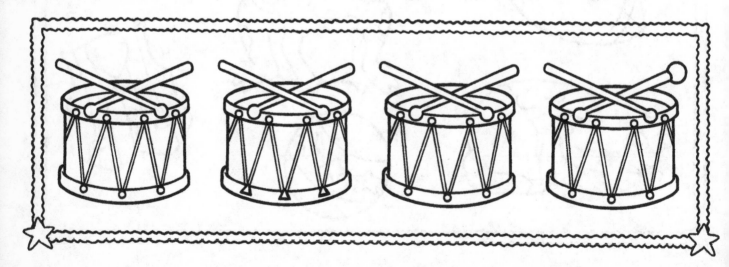

Circle the 2 tops in the row that are exactly alike.
Then circle the 2 Jack-in-the-boxes that are the
same, and the 2 drums that are exactly alike.

34

What did the Three Little Pigs use to build their houses? Unscramble each set of letters and write the words in the blanks.

g q a d w t c a b c l o
p u a d m b a a r m l i
f a b a e l o o n d l n
a c f w o o l g m o o k
b k p n w t r a a m e i

quack   oink   meow   moo   baa

These barnyard animals make lots of sounds!
Each sound is spelled out in the puzzle. Find each
one and circle it. The words go across and down.

Pets are so much fun! But they also need lots of care and attention. Do you have a favorite pet? Draw a picture of it at the end of the leash.

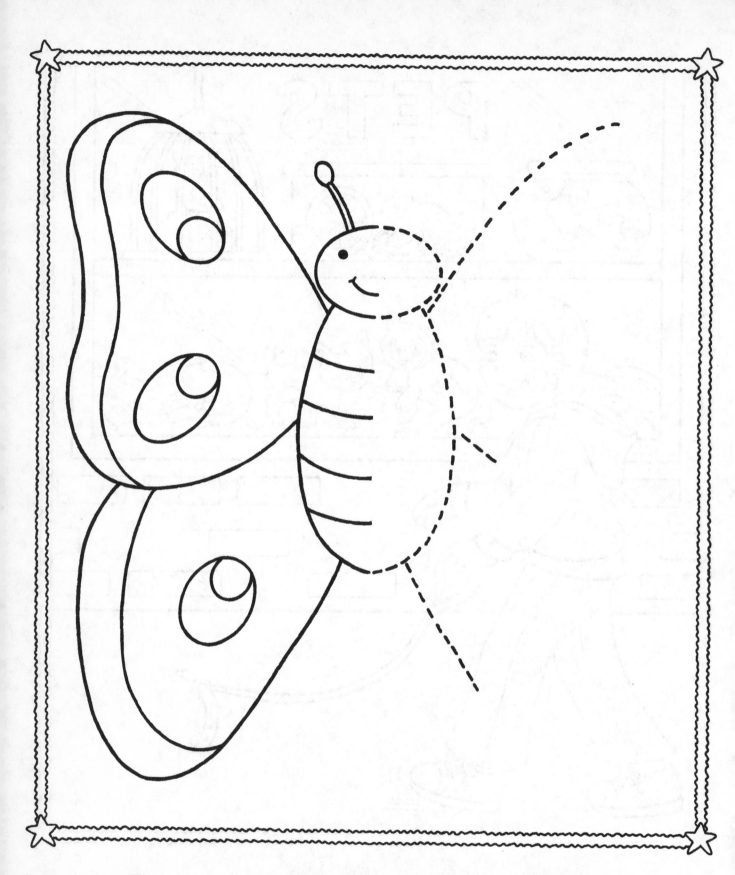

This poor butterfly is missing half of its body and wings! Won't you draw in the rest of the butterfly so it can fly away?

The snow is falling, so let's build one of these! To
see its picture, connect the dots from 1 to 22.

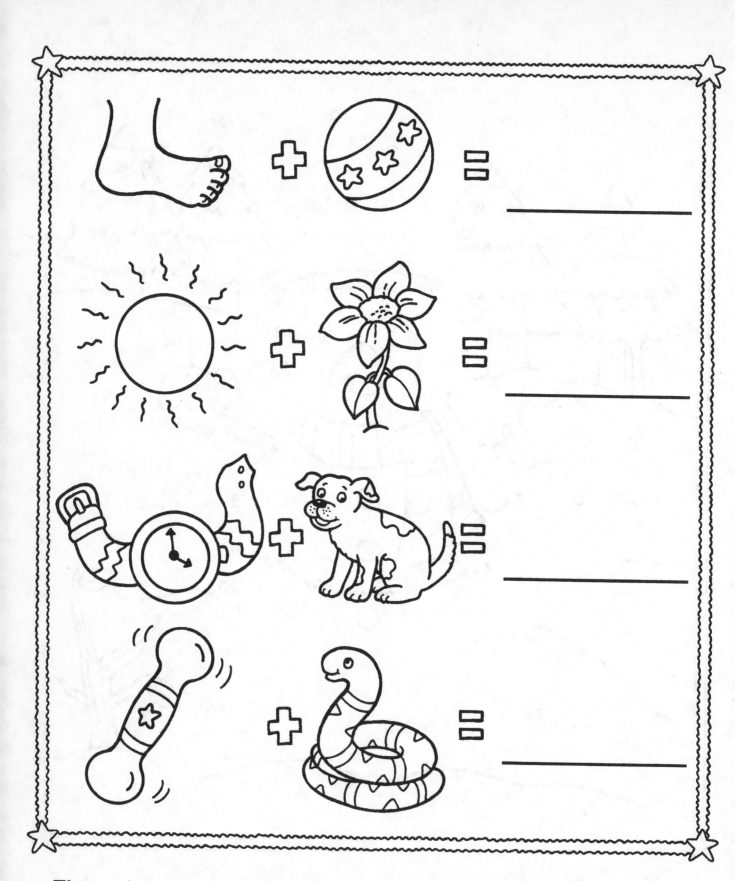

The pictures in each pair, added together, make a new word. Figure out the words for each pair and write the new word in the blank.

START

END

The Three Bears went for a long walk. Now they need to get back to their cottage. Please show them the right path to take to get there.

What has seven colors and appears in the sky?

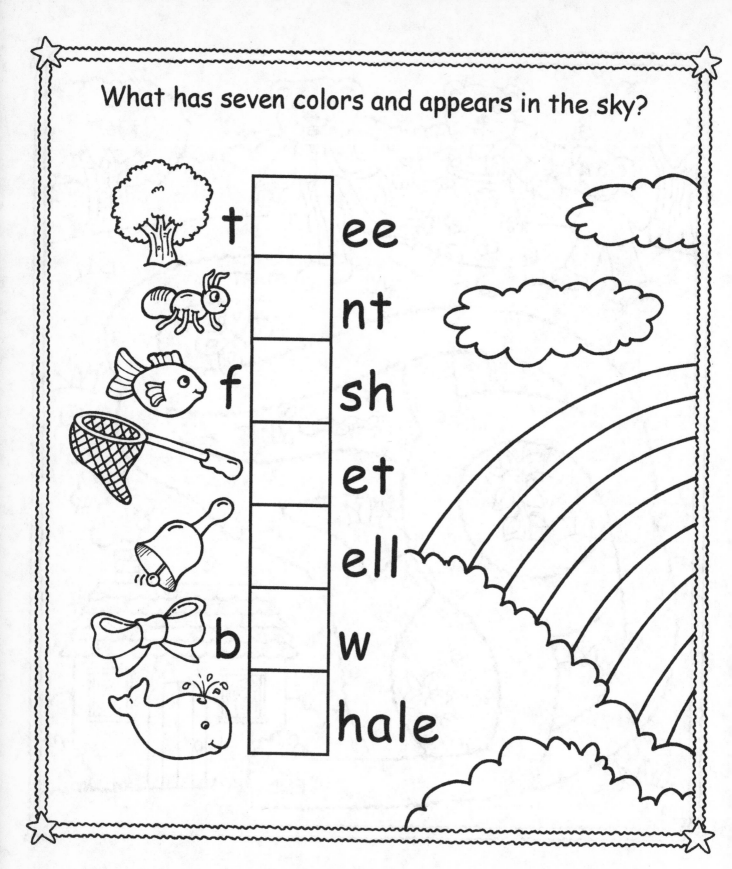

t [ ] ee

[ ] nt

f [ ] sh

[ ] et

[ ] ell

b [ ] w

[ ] hale

To answer the question, fill in a letter to spell the name of each picture. Then read the word you have made from top to bottom.

RED

ORANGE

YELLOW

GREEN

BLUE

INDIGO

VIOLET

Here are 7 colors that might appear in a rainbow. You can make your own rainbow by coloring in the bands. Indigo is a shade of dark blue.

END

START

The little bird wants to get back to her family in the nest at the top of the tree. Please help her by showing her the right path.

Follow the directions for each row of pictures.
Circle the elephant on the LEFT, the cat on
the RIGHT, and the duck in the MIDDLE.

2 down

4 across

d u c k

1 down

3 across

5 across

Complete the puzzle by using the picture clues. Write each word where it belongs in the puzzle. One word has been done for you.

1 down

3 across

2 down

4 across

5 across

The numbers tell you where the
words go in the puzzle.

It's time for a picnic! Circle the things that you eat at a
picnic. Put an X on the things that you would not eat.
Then draw pictures of your favorite foods on the table.

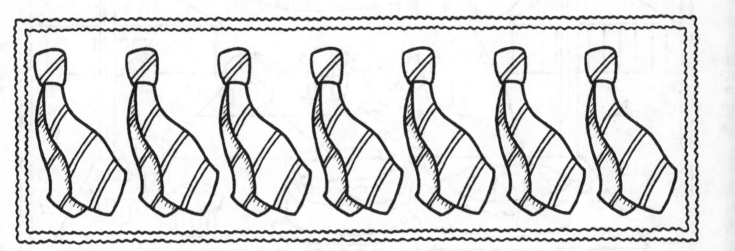

Color 3 kittens orange and 2 kittens gray.
Color 2 ties green and 5 ties red. Color
3 crayons yellow, 3 pink, and 4 purple.

Max has set up a booth at the fair with lots of treats! This picture looks a lot like the one on the opposite page, doesn't it?

Now look at this picture. There are 6 changes. Find and circle the 6 things that are different.

Y A D H T R I B

What does everyone celebrate once a year?
The answer is written backwards. Write the letters
in the opposite order in the balloons.

Solutions

page 4

What kind of fish do dogs chase?

◇ = a ■ = h ● = f ⚡ = t
▲ = c ☆ = i ♥ = s

c a t f i s h
▲ ◇ ⚡ ● ☆ ♥ ■

What runs, but never gets out of breath?

◇ = a ⚡ = t ◉ = e ▮ = w ☾ = r

w a t e r
▮ ◇ ⚡ ◉ ☾

page 5

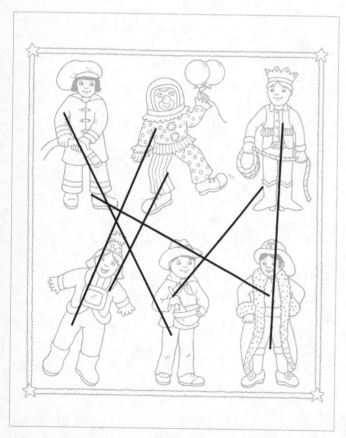

page 6

page 7

page 8

page 9

cake   candle   balloon

page 10

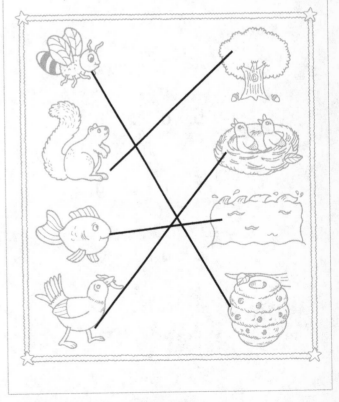

page 11

page 12

What is a large group of fish called?

s	un
c	k
h	eart
o	ne
o	ll
l	

du**c**k

heart

b**o**ne

d**o**ll

pai**l**

page 13

			1 down	
			s	
			u	
2 across	3 down		n	
b	a	r	n	
			o	
4 across			s	
f	r	o	g	
			s	
5 across			t	
c	a	t	e	r

page 14

START

12¢

END

page 16

56

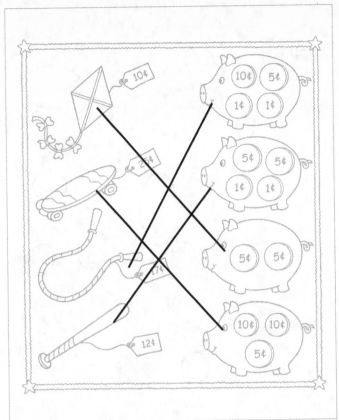

page 17

page 18

page 20

page 21

page 23

page 25

page 26

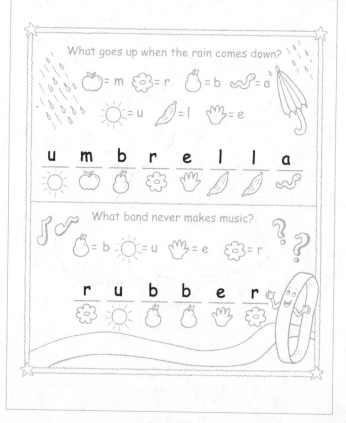

page 28

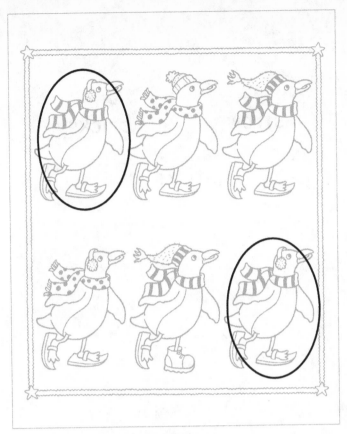

page 29

page 30

page 32

page 33

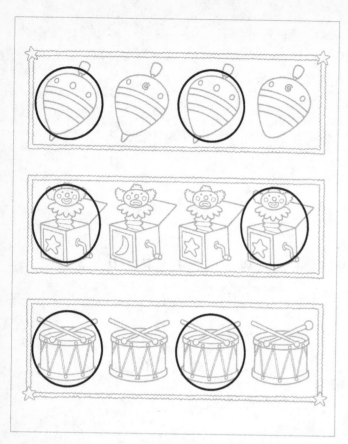

page 34

page 35

page 36

page 39

+ = football

+ = sunflower

+ = watchdog

+ = rattlesnake

page 40

page 41

What has seven colors and appears in the sky?

t	**r** ee
	a nt
f	**i** sh
	n et
	b ell
b	**o** w
	w hale

page 42

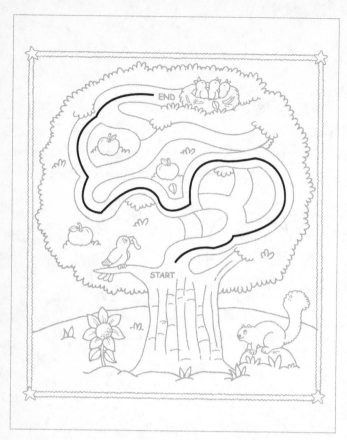

page 44

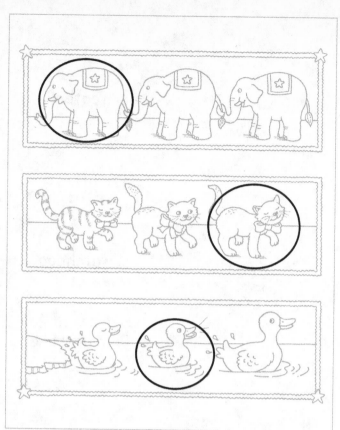

page 45

page 46

page 48

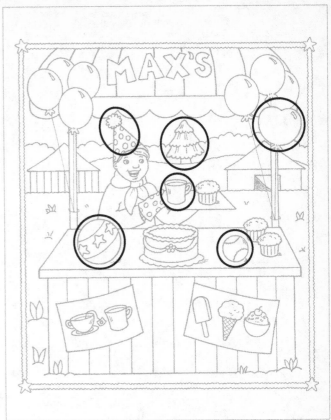

page 51

page 52